VICTORIA & ALBERT
MUSEUM

ALFRED STEVENS
1817–75

SUSAN BEATTIE

LONDON
1975

Front cover Alfred Stevens
From a photograph in the Graves Art Gallery

£1·50p

Printed in England by W. S. Cowell Ltd, Butter Market, Ipswich Dd 094934 K12

ISBN 0 901486 88 4

FOREWORD

On May Day of this year, a century will have passed since the death of one of the most original but enigmatic of all Victorian artists, Alfred Stevens – sculptor, painter, decorator, designer of stoves, grates, fenders, furniture, silverwork, and even lamp-posts, a dabbler in architecture, and a superb draughtsman.

It is right that the Victoria and Albert Museum should commemorate Stevens's death by holding a special exhibition. Not only did he design tables and pewter beer-mugs for use in the Museum's refreshment rooms, but his sculpture and drawings began to enter the collections within a year or two of his death. Equally important are Stevens's pupils, Godfrey Sykes, James Gamble and Reuben Townroe, who were employed from the early 1860s as decorative artists on the older portion of the Museum's buildings, as well as on the Science Schools and the Royal Albert Hall, where his influence is still very apparent. Much of this decoration has subsequently been swept away or hidden, but any visitor to the Victoria and Albert Museum can still see their major joint contribution, the terracotta and mosaic work around the Museum's astounding quadrangle. Perhaps the most spectacular scheme is the Refreshment Room, with its stained glass, white and ochre tiled walls and columns, and painted enamelled iron ceilings, all designed by James Gamble. This room has been closed for nearly forty years, but it is now being restored and will be reopened during 1975 in honour of Alfred Stevens, who inspired it. This is the first of a series of projects to restore certain areas of the Museum to their Victorian splendour.

To mark the centenary of the artist's death, most of his drawings and sculpture at the Tate Gallery are being transferred to this Museum.

I am indebted to Mrs Susan Beattie, who, whilst extremely busy producing the catalogue of the Alfred Stevens drawings in the RIBA Drawings Collection, has written this account of his life and work. She has also, willingly and generously, spared even more time to advise and help, with the assistance of John Physick, on the selection and organisation of the Commemorative Exhibition, in which she has been assisted by Michael Darby and Martin Chapman of the Department of Prints and Drawings.

ROY STRONG
Director
April 1975

INTRODUCTION

During his lifetime and throughout the century since his death, a wide and damaging gulf has separated the few who have found in Alfred Stevens the greatest genius of English sculpture and those to whom he has remained quite unknown or, at best, the obscure author of a large memorial to the Duke of Wellington in St Paul's Cathedral. Awe-inspiring in his total dedication to work and aloof, not only through natural shyness but through a deep sense of purpose in an age of confusion in art, Stevens commanded the complete devotion of those close to him. His pupils called him 'the Master' and the most obsequious of them all, Hugh Stannus, unconsciously set the tone for too many later commentators when, in his biography *Alfred Stevens and his Work* of 1891, he played Vasari to Stevens's Michelangelo. A just analysis of his achievement cannot be made till the whole development of English sculpture and design in the nineteenth and early twentieth centuries is a great deal better known. It is, however, already quite clear that he was not the isolated figure he once appeared to be, but the inspiration and fountain-head of a remarkable revival of sculpture in this country.

Stevens was born in Blandford Forum, Dorset, on 31 December 1817. His father, a man given to hard drinking who put heavy stresses on his wife and family, was a painter with a brisk but essentially local business in heraldic work, shop signs and house decoration. Some of the sketches that Stevens produced as a child – those, for example, in the Dorset County Museum – appear to show the influence of this background with their flat crude shapes and colours that display no astonishingly precocious talent (pl. 1). He seems, however, to have developed at an early age that single-minded devotion to art which was to set him apart from his contemporaries for the rest of his life. It is difficult to imagine what else could have persuaded his parents to allow him to set out from Southampton in the autumn of 1833, alone and not yet 16 years old, to study in Italy on £150 contributed by friends (pl. 2). Stannus was able only to hint at the boy's means of survival during the first of the nine years he was to spend there. Sketching portraits in exchange for board and lodging was one recourse: copying old masters and selling them to unsuspecting dealers as originals was another. He was attached informally to the Academy in Florence for most of the time, but learnt more by travelling about the country observing, sketching and copying – by total immersion in painting, sculpture and architecture of the Renaissance (pl. 10). Not until 1841 did he at last take the traditional step of entering an artist's studio as an assistant. His choice of master was the neo-classical sculptor Bertel Thorwaldsen, whose studio in Rome was at that time among the most renowned in the capital. When, in 1842, Thorwaldsen went home to Denmark for the last time, Stevens decided to return to England.

His growth as an artist between 1834 and 1842 is summarised in the contrast between the nervous little figures that fill the sketchbook dating from his earliest years in Italy now in the Royal Institute of British Architects Drawing Collection, and the brilliantly economical and vigorous drawings that he began to make, probably shortly before his return home, in preparation for a series of illustrations to the *Iliad* and *Odyssey*, now principally in an album in the Ashmolean Museum, Oxford. These reveal the extent of Thorwaldsen's influence as no other drawings do; they also betray something of that harshly disciplined working method which Stevens learnt from the sculptor and followed ever after, often at the expense of spontaneity in the finished work and, always, of his own peace of mind.

The rest of that year was probably spent in a state of restless anticipation in Blandford, as Stevens and his family once again discussed his future and how best he should set about establishing himself as an artist. Two of the first things he undertook were portraits, one of his friend Alfred Pegler (pl. 8), and one of a Mr Bennett of Blandford, a lost work recorded in Stevens's letters to the Peglers and probably the first commission he ever received in England. He was also, it seems, given an opportunity to help his father with the decoration of an interior: the staircase hall at Chettle House, near Blandford, where George Stevens was employed in the early 1840s, still contains five relief panels copied assiduously from reliefs by Thorwaldsen now in the Thorwaldsen Museum, Copenhagen.

Perhaps Stevens's reluctance to do more than reproduce the work of his master at this time reflects his preoccupation with the important Government competition, announced in the spring of 1842 with a closing date in June 1843, for which he had decided to enter. This was the first of several competitions intended to discover fresco painters for the new Houses of Parliament. Stevens's cartoon, a roundel with a scene from Milton's *Paradise Lost* framed by four spandrel panels of crouching angels (pl. 3) to form a square, was unplaced in the awards and coolly described by the *Art Union* as 'A number of headlong figures, grouped circularly, as if designed for a bas-relief . . .'

The second competition, in which artists were required to submit actual specimens of fresco painting, provided the impetus for Stevens, undaunted by his earlier failure, to leave Blandford for London early in 1844 and take lodgings at 10 Robert Street in the Hampstead Road. His struggle to produce a fresco panel 3 feet wide by 2 feet 5 inches high to meet the closing date in June and, indeed, even to survive on nothing but a small loan from Samuel Pegler, is pitifully apparent in the first letters he wrote from Robert Street to the Pegler family:

'At my study I am almost at a stand for want of materials, besides which the feeling of poverty and dread of being dunned for certain small bills that I had promised to pay some day soon, have anything but a favourable effect on my painting.

'I feel quite ashamed that my first letter to you should be of this character. I should have written before, but I have excuses that might serve a man more attentive to these things than myself. I have had nothing interesting to tell you and I have been so constantly employed. I cannot afford to have workmen so that I have to do everything even to sifting the sand and making mortar myself. When I leave my study at night (I work from 7 till 2) I am so tired that after dining I can do nothing I am too glad to go to bed.'

Yet the robust optimism of the last paragraph of this letter seems quite spontaneous, 'You will be glad to hear', he told Samuel Pegler, 'that my chances of complete success [in the competition] are even greater than I had supposed before leaving Blandford. I have only to pray that the judges be neither rogues nor fools . . .'

Sadly, his hopes of success were quite unfounded. He did, at least, receive a moderately discerning comment from the *Art Union*, whose critic found the style of his fresco composition, a scene from *Richard III*, to be 'imitated from the Giotteschi. The composition consists of three female figures, the centre one of which is deduced from some one of the most devout of the ancient masters, and not a very fitting impersonation for a scene from Shakespeare. The work exhibits some power, nevertheless; the artist may have a fertile imagination, and possess some skill in depicting character. He seems also to have studied the frescoes of the old masters.' A faded photograph is the only record of this work to survive apart from a few preliminary drawings (pl. 4).

Considering that Stevens was at the start of his career, unknown and with scarcely any commissioned work to show, it was a remarkable stroke of good fortune that, probably through a contact first made in Italy, he was asked in 1845 to provide examples of his architectural drawings with a view to obtaining a post in 'Architecture, Perspective and Modelling' at the Government School of Design at Somerset House (pl. 41). 'I was offered a place . . . as *Professor of everything*', he wrote to Alfred Pegler, adding conspiratorially, 'I am to be smuggled in by what trick I cannot tell'. His appointment to do five hours of teaching daily at a salary of £150 year and to instruct in 'Painting and Ornament if required', brought Stevens face to face with the subject of design in industry, over which a battle had been raging on a national scale for several years. The industrial revolution had caught English artists unawares: suddenly it was apparent that countless objects of everyday use were being produced to an appallingly low standard of design and those in authority were panicked into deciding that a new generation of students must be taught, not Art, but Design, in order to supply the manufacturers' need. Schools of Design were inaugurated throughout the country following the Government Committee on Arts and Manufactures in 1836, but ten years later were still failing to relate their teaching programme to the demands of industry. 'They have been lately so lashed by the press as incompetent', wrote Stevens of the authorities at Somerset House, '. . . that they tremble for their places and are very happy to find me knowing a little of what they ought to understand well themselves.' The truth was that Stevens, though grateful enough to find employment as a result of these Government measures was, and remained, wholly scornful of the idea behind them: that design could be taught as a subject quite distinct from painting, sculpture and architecture. He had the opportunity to make his opinion clear in 1847 when he appeared before a special committee investigating the management of the Somerset House school. He was examined closely on his experience of art education in Italy. Was there a class of design in the Florentine Academy? None at all. What, then, was the course of instruction pursued by decorative artists or designers? 'The pupils', he assured the committee, 'were all educated as if they intended to become artists. After having finished their education some may become painters of rooms, but their education up to the time they leave the school is conducted as if they intended to be artists.'

Later he admitted, 'It is very difficult to compare the School at Somerset House with so complete an Institution as the Florentine Academy'. Tired of the bickering and discontent at Somerset House, Stevens left his job there towards the end of 1847. He had found, too, that the obligation to spend five hours there daily was far more disruptive to his own work than he had anticipated.

Potentially, at least, the most important work to result directly from his employment at the School was the design for the doorcase and panel decoration of massive bronze doors for the newly built Geological Museum in Jermyn Street, Piccadilly (pl. 5). Stevens gained the commission through the recommendation of C. H. Wilson, Director at Somerset House, who had been asked by the Museum's Director, Henry de la Beche, to name a suitable candidate. Wilson's letter, dated 7 December 1847, introducing Stevens as 'the best Artist in London for the purpose', is now in the National Museum of Wales and is one of the few pieces of evidence found recently that illuminates Stevens's obscure early years. A payment of £20 is all that he appears to have received for the design when, it must be presumed, shortage of funds delayed and finally prohibited the execution of the doors. They were to have been cast in high relief with panels containing figures symbolising the minerals iron, coal, gold and stone, and scenes of action depicting men forging, mining and quarrying (pl. 6). The preparatory sketches, mostly for nude figures in the forge scene, are remarkably close to some of the drawings of Thorwaldsen, while the final design in the Victoria and Albert Museum is a key to all the most powerful guiding forces that Stevens had found in the Italian Renaissance, from Giotto to Donatello and Signorelli, from Raphael to Michelangelo. The same synthesis of quattrocento delicacy and heroic grandeur is evident in his design for the interior decoration of the Geological Museum, two drawings for which have recently been discovered in the archives of the present Museum at South Kensington. Painted niches, shown between the windows overlooking Piccadilly, frame figures of Raphaelesque power but are bordered by bands and panels that echo the prettiness of a Rossellino tomb (pl. 7).

Stevens is not known to have undertaken any other sculptural project before 1850, except, that is, for a brief attempt to redesign the base of Nelson's Column and certain designs for metalwork that are discussed below. Many of the projects begun during the period 1842–50 were of his own devising – exercises in composition with which he must eventually have grown weary and abandoned or destroyed. Nothing approaching a finished work has ever been found for the portrait of a young woman represented in sketches at the Royal Institute of British Architects (pl. 9) and Princeton University Art Museum, for the composition 'Moses and the Brazen Serpent', 'Parmigiano painting during the Sack of Rome' and the mysterious subject known as the 'Struggling Figures' (pl. 66), for all of which large numbers of studies survive. A panel painting of the Ascension of Christ is extant, in an incomplete and ruinous condition, at the Fitzwilliam Museum, Cambridge (pls. 11, 12). A series of Bible illustrations in pen and ink was begun about 1848, giving him the opportunity to use his intimate knowledge of Italianate decoration and to experiment with the same range of subjects that had frequently preoccupied his masters (pl. 13). Some of Stevens's loveliest early drawings are among this Bible series: his inability or unwillingness to complete it is one of the more irksome of his failures. Only in the roundel composition 'King Alfred and his Mother', for which two oil sketches on panel exist, did Stevens bring himself close to producing a finished work (pl. 37).

Three schemes of painted decoration belong to the period. The first, the decoration of part of Sir Robert Peel's townhouse, 3 Whitehall Gardens, was a group undertaking of pupils and masters at Somerset House, for which L. W. Collmann, the interior decorator brought in by Peel's architect Sydney Smirke, received all the credit. Nothing of this but a few drawings by Stevens for ceiling panels survives. The second scheme, intended for a billiard room at 30 Westbourne Terrace in Paddington, is known through a series of sketches divided principally between the Tate Gallery and Princeton University Art Museum, and a final design for the ceiling decoration, now in the Victoria and Albert Museum (pls. 14, 15). The scenes from Homer that border the round-ended ceiling are conceived in the most gentle and lyrical of Sartoesque manners: they became a kind of compendium of ideas for compositions and figure poses to which Stevens would return again and again when working on other schemes. The 'Homecoming of Odysseus' panel, to take the most obvious example, was reused as a whole in the decoration of a mantelpiece frieze for a friend in Sheffield in 1851, while many details foreshadow those of the third decorative scheme carried out before 1850 at Deysbrook, near Liverpool, the most important of its kind and the longest to remain *in situ* (pls. 16, 17). The decorator in charge of work at the house was Leonard Collmann. Whether Sir Robert Peel's house had been the scene of the first meeting between him and Stevens is not known, but it seems most probable that the artist's employment at Deysbrook was a result of the favourable impression he had made on Collmann on that occasion. It was the first of a series of commissions to contribute to schemes in the charge of the firm of Collmann & Davis. So far as is known, Stevens did not fail to complete any job where he was answerable to the firm. The dining-room and drawing-rooms at Deysbrook survived resplendent with their lacy grotesques and figure panels of consummate elegance until 1946, when the house was demolished. The principal panels and examples of the border decoration were taken into store at the Walker Art Gallery, Liverpool.

In 1850 occurred one of those dramatic changes of direction which punctuate the phases of Stevens's development: he left London to become chief designer to the firm of Hoole & Co, of Sheffield, ironfounders and manufacturers of stoves, grates and fenders. His previous contacts with manufacturers are undocumented and Stannus names only one firm, William Potts of Birmingham, for whom, he states, Stevens designed candlesticks 'for the Great Exhibition'. But, according to Henry Hoyles, who had himself worked for Hoole for many years and remembered Stevens well, the artist had produced these candlestick designs as specimens of his work when first introduced to Henry Hoole; that is, before 1850. Late in 1847 he wrote to Alfred Pegler, 'I am now working very hard at something for the forthcoming Exhibition': surely a reference, not to the 1851 Exhibition at that early date, but to one of the annual exhibitions of decorative art held at the Society of Arts from 1847 to 1850; the 'something' perhaps being the candlesticks themselves, though the Society's catalogues reveal nothing to connect Stevens with the exhibits of William Potts (pl. 18).

In contrast to so much of Stevens's life, his activity as a designer of metalwork for Hoole's from 1850 to 1857 is well documented, from the moment of his introduction to Hoole by Young Mitchell, one of his former pupils at Somerset House and now, in 1849, head of the School of Art in Sheffield. The principal sources are the notes, now in the Royal Institute of British Architects MS Collection, made by Stannus probably on site at Hoole's factory, during the preparation of the biography, and a transcript, in the Graves Art Gallery, Sheffield, of 'Alfred Stevens's salary a/c at Green Lane Works . . . 1850–57'. The first payment – an advance of £50 – was made to the artist on 28 February 1850 and on 16 March settlement was made for the carriage of two boxes to Sheffield – presumably Stevens's luggage. Up to 21 December 1850 the total amount paid to him was £229 and by 5 September 1851 he had received a further £200. After that date all payments were made to him in London, where, in the autumn of 1851, he had taken a lease of 7 Canning Place, Kensington. The period of some twenty months spent at Hoole's Green Lane Works in Sheffield was in some respects the most productive of Stevens's life. His feeling for the casting method and the nature of the materials with which he had to work, for colour and, above all, for sculptural quality, were to gain for the firm of Hoole a reputation for fine products second to none in the mid-nineteenth century. When Stevens arrived in Sheffield all manufacturers were preparing for the Great Exhibition due to open in May 1851, and he was set to work immediately on a series of fire grates, stoves and fenders to fill Hoole's stand in the Crystal Palace. Two of the most beautiful pieces he designed for the occasion are the Hot Air Stove (pl. 19) and the 'Boy' Stove, both represented in the Museum. Stevens's delay in finishing the *putti* in high relief, which give the latter stove its name and support garlands set into the semi-circular surround, provoked the splendidly irate letter written by Henry Hoole to his works in Sheffield on 25 April 1851, which is now among the Stannus Papers in the Royal Institute of British Architects. 'The Exhibition', he stormed, *'will be opened* on the 1st May and on *Tuesday* next the Queen is to have a private View – Stevens must therefore without any mistake let me have the Boys here on Monday. – He has not acted the part of a high minded man of feeling & honor in his transactions with me – I have had the mortification of seeing a number of his designs for large knives, Handles & blades, which the party boasts will be here finished by the 30th Inst & our own work is – where? This surely is not correct in principle, or in accordance with the agreement he entered into with me, nor does it show much consideration for the feelings – outraged as they have been so often by his neglect – or failure or anything else you like to call it – but I certainly was not prepared to find that he had been bartering our interests, & honor, by selling his time for a paltry sum of Twenty pounds – O Temporae! O Mores !! You know well how gladly I would have given him £50. 0. 0. if he had only enabled us to have stood far above competition, how pleased I should have been to show my satisfaction in a thousand ways, if he had not so often mortified me by compelling me as a suitor, to entreat as a precious boon, what it was his duty to have offered without solicitation . . .' Somewhat mollified, Hoole added in a postscript that he had seen 'no Air Stoves equal to Stevens' – as well he might, for his exhibits were declared by the Jury to be 'among the most remarkable contributions from the United Kingdom', and were in no way overshadowed, as Hoole had feared, by the knives and sheaths Stevens had designed for the rival firm of George Wostenholm (pl. 20).

The stoves and grates of Hoole & Co were awarded the Council Medal in Class XXII, Iron and General Hardware. An even greater triumph was achieved at the Paris Universal Exhibition in 1855 when the exhibits of Hoole and Stevens were transferred on the grounds of superior merit from Class IX (Heat, Light and Electricity) to Class XXIV (Furniture and Decoration), winning for their manufacturer a Medal of Honour and for their designer a collaborating artist's Silver Medal. 'Thanks to the genius of Mr Alfred Stevens', wrote Matthew Digby Wyatt as juror, 'this branch of trade has been developed to such an extent, as to have obtained the suffrage of all nations and to have won for the house of Hoole the distinguished reward of a gold medal of honour . . . What especially gratified the French connoisseurs was to observe that good taste presided equally over the designs for the cheapest and for the most expensive goods produced by the house' (pls. 21, 24, 25). One of the most popular pieces was the so-called 'Pluto and Proserpine' grate, designed in 1855 probably expressly for the Paris Exhibition, and known to have been exhibited and acclaimed in London at the International Exhibition of 1862 (pl. 22). Resplendent with concave fireback decorated in low relief with a scene of the Rape of Proserpine, with fender and firedogs of the most lavish and complex design, the grate epitomises Stevens's conception of the household object as a complete work of art, no part overlooked or thought less worthy of attention than another, the whole subject to rigorous classical standards of beauty and proportion. The bronze 'figure dogs' of 1852–3 and their accompanying grate with elegant stove cheeks show with equally dramatic effect the new dimension that Stevens gave to the ordinary (pl. 23). Who else in the mid-nineteenth century could have invented a firedog that derived from the *ignudi* of the Sistine Chapel ceiling and yet was wholly fitting to its purpose? The experience of working for Hoole had, in turn, a liberating effect upon Stevens. Now for the first and last time in his life, virtually every design he produced was followed through at a reasonable speed and realised in a finished work which was then put on the market at no further trouble to himself. No sooner did the link with Hoole slacken in 1856–7 than he lost the impetus to design for industry in a disciplined and productive manner. It must have seemed insanely wasteful to those manufacturers anxious to employ him that, though he continued to spend a great deal of his own time in designing silver and majolica ware, street furniture and stove grates, he would often refuse to enter into business dealings with them (pls. 28, 29, 31). He flatly declined, in 1856, to allow the Atkins brothers, silversmiths of Sheffield, to buy any of his designs for silverware. He sold two chimney-piece designs to the Coalbrookdale Iron Company at about the same time but, pleased though the firm was with them, would undertake no more (pls. 26, 27). He declined, too, to alter in any detail the two designs that he did consent to make for

Joseph Bradbury, a silver table-centre and a tray. An entertaining letter from Bradbury to Stannus, preserved in the Royal Institute of British Architects, describes the faults of these two pieces, one with branches so designed that, when its candles were lit, the flowers caught fire, the other so heavy as to be almost impossible to lift. It is evident that a strong element of impatience had begun to infect his attitude to manufacturers by 1856. His last recorded works for a manufacturer were the designs he made for Minton of Stoke-on-Trent, for a large and small vase and a dinner and dessert plate, c. 1861 (pl. 30). Perhaps he felt that the versatility upon which he set such great value had been threatened by his commitment to Hoole. And indeed, though Stevens produced his most notable portrait paintings during the period 1850–6 – the Mrs Mitchell and Child, the Leonard and Mary Ann Collmann of c. 1854 (pls. 32, 33) – an alarming number of the decorative schemes projected in those years had come to nothing. Of those that were realised, only one, a series of unimpressive ceiling panels in Harewood House, Yorkshire, survives today.

In 1852 Stevens assisted with the decoration of the Italian Court in the Crystal Palace, then recently re-erected at Sydenham (pl. 35). Shortly afterwards he was making sketches for the decoration of the boudoir at Daylesford House, Gloucestershire, but there is no indication that the scheme was taken further (pl. 34). Plans for elaborate ceiling paintings in a private waiting-room at Paddington Station for the use of Queen Victoria occupied him in 1854 but were laid aside for lack of funds (pl. 36). What must have been the most successful of his smaller schemes, the decoration, under the auspices of L. W. Collmann, of the drawing-room at 11 Kensington Palace Gardens with ten canvas panels depicting Heroines from Spenser's *Faerie Queene*, disappeared without trace early this century (pl. 38).

The grandest programme of decoration Stevens devised before 1856 was that for the dome of the British Museum's Reading Room, but once again his ambitious plans were far beyond the means of the authorities (pl. 39). Though apparently quite incapable of making concessions to economy and expediency, Stevens was championed on this and many other occasions by men of influence and it is impossible not to suspect that a great many more of his schemes would have been carried out if he had only moderated, in his sketch designs at least, the awesome grandeur of his conceptions. As it was, Sir Anthony Panizzi's attempts to persuade the Museum's Trustees to give the Reading Room a fitting decoration fell on obstinately deaf ears and the great expanse of the dome received in the end plain coats of paint in blue, white and gold.

One other project which belongs to the period deserves mention here as the first of the two major architectural schemes upon which Stevens is known to have embarked. The competition for a new School of Art for Sheffield, announced in 1854, naturally attracted his interest for he had been living and working in the town when plans for building a new school were first being discussed. His entry received no recognition in the Committee's report and was probably too incomplete even to receive serious consideration. Nothing approaching a finished drawing has yet been found, though the series of studies in the Royal Institute of

British Architects Drawings Collection, mainly showing an impossibly rich and grandiose elevation in the manner of an Italian Renaissance palace, is the most coherent body of Stevens's architectural work to have survived (pl. 40).

1856, like 1850, was a crucial turning point in Stevens's development, the year in which he was unknowingly to commit the rest of his life to his two master-pieces, the decoration of the dining-room of Dorchester House and the Wellington Monument for St Paul's Cathedral. The story of the monument, from the com-petition in which Stevens was at first placed joint fifth with five other entrants, and his foolhardy promise in 1857 to provide a full-size model *and* the finished work for only a fraction of the originally allocated cost, to his hounding by govern-ment officials until his death eighteen years later and the final completion of the memorial in 1912, is among the most scandalous, tragic and intriguing stories in English art. The monument itself, towering in the Cathedral nave, seems now to be the very embodiment of Stevens's perplexing and melancholy genius. Awk-ward and heavy as an architectural whole, it reflects the painfully laborious process of trial and retrial, revision and modification that the drawings of the structural parts also betray, yet the individual parts are unsurpassed in English sculpture. The sarcophagus on its elaborate base, carrying the recumbent figure of the Duke, is close to the eye of the beholder and minutely detailed, encrusted with delicate ornament. Outflung from their plinths far above, are the heroic figure groups of Truth and Falsehood, Valour and Cowardice, which, with their fluid surfaces and largeness of outline, perfectly acknowledge their lofty position and, dynamic in their interaction, lose nothing of their power whatever view-point is taken from the nave or aisle below. Worked in bronze, these figures are Stevens's noblest achievement as a sculptor: their influence on the following generation of British sculptors was immediate and profound (pls. 42–46).

When Robert Stainer Holford commissioned Stevens in about 1855 to decorate rooms in his Park Lane mansion, Dorchester House, newly completed to the designs of Lewis Vulliamy, he little knew to what anxieties and agonising delays he and his wife were doomed. In a letter to Stannus written in the nineties he wistfully recalled how he had told Stevens at the beginning that he wanted, not 'high art' but a normal decorator's job at a reasonable cost. What he received, by the slowest degrees in the course of some fifteen years and at a cost of about £8,000, was a dining-room with furnishings of the utmost splendour but still lacking any painted decoration, a monumental marble chimney-piece for the saloon, and doors into the gallery on the *piano nobile* with carved medallions of great beauty – all expressive of the most potent drive imaginable to create 'high' art in the spirit of the Medicis. When at last, about 1869, the chimney-piece was installed in the saloon, and Holford had received the bill for it, he could not forbear to comment, '. . . had I known that the saloon chimneypiece would have cost so large a sum as £1,800 I should have been content with a good form and much less ornament, while admiring its beauty . . .' The caryatid chimney-piece designed for the dining-room ranks with the Wellington Monument figure groups as Stevens's finest sculptural work. The magnificent crouching female figures that bear the entablature blocks of the mantelshelf are of white marble and were finished after 1875 by the artist's pupil, James Gamble, with perhaps a too zealous regard for highly polished surfaces: their robust and compactly balanced forms are the final refinement of an idea which can be observed at every stage of its development in Stevens's sketches and models and which, as some of the more furiously worked sheets clearly show, he carried to the point of an obsession (pls. 47–52).

But for the Dorchester House commission 1856–8 would have been bleak and disappointing years. The final result of the Wellington Monument competition was not made public until 1858 and meanwhile Stevens had entered and failed in three competitions in quick succession: a limited competition in February 1856 to design two prize medals for the Department of Science and Art (pl. 67), a competition for the Government Offices in September, and one for the memorial to the Great Exhibition in July 1857 (pls. 53, 54).

Early in 1858 he moved from Canning Place, Kensington, to a rented cottage near Walham Green, Hammersmith – a puzzling development for there is reason to suppose that he was by this time thinking of designing a house for himself. As soon as the Wellington Monument became his responsibility in September he was in need of some property, however temporary, that would be large enough to shelter the full-size model. A disused church on the corner of Eton Villas and Church (now Eton) Road off Haverstock Hill in Hampstead appeared to serve the purpose admirably and of this he took a seven-year lease from October 1858. It cannot have taken Stevens long to realise that here at last was the opportunity to build his own house and studio. He began to make sketches of a massive mansion based at first on the framework of the church, in which, meanwhile, the model of the Monument was slowly taking shape, and where certain basic alterations were already in progress to make the structure habitable in the short term. It is probable that he had left York Cottage and was actually living in the church by early 1860, under what circumstances of discomfort it is barely possible to imagine. By September 1862, however, he had moved, as a temporary measure, into 9 Eton Villas, a small house in the nearby terrace, in which he lived for the rest of his life. Reluctant to abandon the idea of keeping the church as his house, Stevens did not acknowledge the move to Eton Villas on his letters until five years later, but kept the address he had invented for the church, 5 Church Road. The new house was up to first storey level at the time of his death. An upper floor was added shortly afterwards and the building survived until 1964, when the site was redeveloped (pl. 55).

Whenever time allowed, Stevens would plan the fittings and furniture that were to fill his 'Italian Casino', as Stannus described it. Conceived in the wake of the Dorchester House commission, the interior was evidently intended to parallel, though in less sumptuous style, many of the features used in Holford's mansion. What little now remains of the furniture that he and his carpenter made seems heartbreakingly far removed from the richly detailed and beautifully finished pieces that the drawings suggest (pl. 56). The panelling for the library-cum-dining-room survives, incomplete and now dismantled, in the Walker Art Gallery, Liverpool. Only the drawing table, also at Liverpool, with its painted door panels and generous scale evokes something of the proud dream he had once cherished.

Whilst the Wellington Monument and Dorchester House absorbed so much of Stevens's time, few of the other projects that engaged his attention after 1858 had any hope of realisation. Potentially the most important decorative scheme he ever devised, to cover the dome of St Paul's Cathedral and its drum and sub-structure with mosaic and sculpture, was suggested to him by F. C. Penrose, Surveyor to the Fabric, in 1862. He constructed a huge half-model of the domed space to show his intentions, which were irresistibly reminiscent of Michelangelo's in the Sistine Chapel, and his design for one of the spandrels, a figure of Isaiah, was carried out in 1864. Various attempts to push the programme further, with or without the help of Stevens, came to nothing until 1888, when the three other spandrel prophets for which he had left adequate drawings and models were executed. Shortly afterwards the whole scheme was forgotten (pls. 57–61).

It would be wrong to blame Stevens himself for the failure of Penrose's scheme for, so far as is known, he never did receive a formal commission from the Dean and Chapter, and seems to have spent a great deal of time in working for nothing on the designs. Lack of documentation, which clouds so many aspects of his life and work, makes it impossible, similarly, to ascertain whether he was asked, or merely undertook for his own interest, about 1859, to make sketches for the arcades of the Horticultural Society's new garden at South Kensington. In the event Sydney Smirke and Stevens's pupil Godfrey Sykes, newly arrived from Sheffield to work for the Department of Science and Art, were together responsible for its architectural form.

The case of Christ Church, Cosway Street, in St Marylebone, where Stevens was asked to provide a painting for the lunette space on the altar wall is the supreme example of the artist's reckless and ultimately fatal disregard of his client's demands. Having decided on the subject of the wall painting – the Annunciation to the Shepherds – Stevens proceeded to make innumerable rough sketches and life studies for each figure in the composition, which he would scribble over and over again in detail and as a whole. According to another of his pupils, Reuben Townroe, who was working with him at the time, c. 1862, the incumbent of Christ Church would call at the studio at regular intervals to enquire after the painting's progress, and each time was turned away with token excuses until he lost patience and abandoned the scheme. *The Annunciation to the Shepherds*, which inspired some of the finest figure drawings that Stevens ever produced, exists in its most complete form as a large oil sketch now in the Tate Gallery (pls. 62, 63).

Stevens is known to have assisted L. W. Collmann with two decorative schemes during the sixties, both of which are now destroyed, but are represented in drawings. The earlier, of c. 1863–4, was the redecoration of the Olympic Theatre, off the Strand (pl. 64), and the second, of 1868, at Melchet Court, Hampshire, for Lady Ashburton. Small design projects included a commission to decorate the cover of the magazine *Once a Week*, for which he made several drawings, but delegated to his pupil, Gamble, an idea for the figure-head and interior fittings of a yacht (pl. 65) and, most notably and successfully, the design for a Certificate of Honourable Mention for use at the International Exhibition of 1862 (pl. 68).

In 1867 Stevens had a serious heart attack and his health rapidly deteriorated thereafter. He took on no new work but sank deeper into himself as the completion of the Monument came to occupy every waking moment. The letters to Alfred Pegler, which have survived in an almost unbroken series from 1864 to 1875, describe a life of constant battle, not only against illness and exhaustion, but against aggressive government officials beginning to despair of the Monument, and his own rapidly growing reputation as an unmanageable and sullen eccentric at the centre of a national scandal. 'You have no doubt seen the preposterous report in the papers about my sanity', he wrote despairingly in April 1873, 'pray contradict this whenever you have a chance – if you wish it I can send down my doctor's certificate – how this blunder came to be made is a story too long for a letter . . .' A final humiliation came when he was forced to borrow money from Pegler, just as he had done thirty years before when he first came young and penniless to London. Yet Stevens's optimism was irrepressible. 'I am hopeful with the new year', he exclaimed in a rare dated letter of 2 January 1875, 'I had a visit yesterday from the Office of Works the gentleman most pleasant & friendly & told me how the foreign sculptors had been saying fine things about my figures' [Truth and Falsehood, Valour and Cowardice]. Five months later, in a state of general debility, his lungs congested, he died during another heart attack on 1 May. 'Thus', ran his obituary in the *Builder*, 'has passed away from us a man, quiet and unobtrusive in his ways, whose influence in Classic Art has been, and will continue to be, very strongly felt, and whose death we cannot speak of as less than a loss to the nation.'

SHORT BIBLIOGRAPHY

Walter Armstrong
Alfred Stevens, a biographical study
1881

Hugh Stannus
Alfred Stevens and his work
1891

H. I. Potter
*Notes on some works by Alfred Stevens from 1850 to 1857 as shown by
the original drawings and models in the possession of
Messrs. Henry Hoole & Co. Ltd. of Green Lane Works, Sheffield*
n.d. [c. 1910]

Kenneth Romney Towndrow
Alfred Stevens, a biography with new material
1939

Kenneth Romney Towndrow
The Works of Alfred Stevens at the Tate Gallery
1950

John Physick
The Wellington Monument
Victoria and Albert Museum
1970

Susan Beattie
R.I.B.A. Drawings Collection, Alfred Stevens
(forthcoming, with a full bibliography)

PRINCIPAL PUBLIC COLLECTIONS
OF ALFRED STEVENS'S WORK

London
British Museum
Royal Institute of British Architects, Drawings Collection
Tate Gallery
Victoria and Albert Museum

Great Britain, except London
Ashmolean Museum, Oxford
City Museum and Art Galleries, Sheffield
Fitzwilliam Museum, Cambridge
National Gallery of Scotland, Edinburgh
Walker Art Gallery, Liverpool

United States of America
Art Museum, Princeton University, New Jersey
Fogg Art Museum, Harvard University, Cambridge, Massachussets

Australia
National Gallery of Victoria, Melbourne

1 Family group
c. 1824
Water-colour
Dorset County Museum

2 View of San
Gimignano
c. 1835
Pencil and water-colour
*Royal Institute of
British Architects*

3 Sketch for spandrel
figure, Houses of Parlia-
ment fresco competition
1842
Black chalk on brown
paper
*Victoria and Albert
Museum*
E.2563–1911

4 Fresco depicting a
scene from *Richard III*.
Houses of Parliament
fresco competition
1843
*From a photograph in
the Royal Institute of
British Architects*

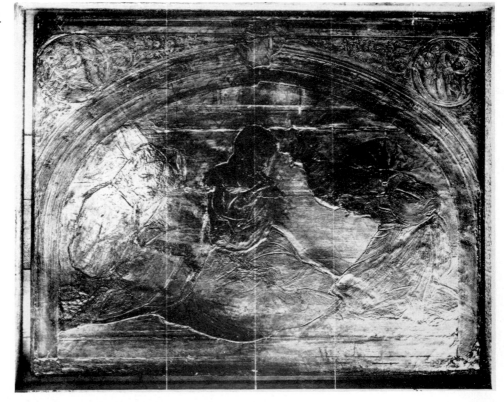

5 Design for the door-
case and bronze doors of
the Geological Museum,
Jermyn Street
1848
Pen and wash
*Victoria and Albert
Museum, 8068*

6 Preparatory sketch
for door panel,
Geological Museum,
Jermyn Street
1848
Red chalk
*Victoria and Albert
Museum, D.2062–1885*

7 Design for the interior
decoration of the
Geological Museum,
Jermyn Street
c. 1848
Water-colour, ink and
pencil
Geological Museum

8 Miniature portrait of
Alfred Pegler
1842
Water-colour on ivory
*Victoria and Albert
Museum, E.351–1975*

9 Study for a portrait
of a young woman
c. 1845–6
Water-colour
*Royal Institute of
British Architects*

10 Copy by Stevens of
Titian's Assumption of
the Virgin
Walker Art Gallery

11 The Ascension of
Christ
c. 1845–6
Oil and gesso on panel
Fitzwilliam Museum

12 Preparatory study
for The Ascension of
Christ
c. 1845–6
Black chalk
*Victoria and Albert
Museum, E.2499–1911*

13 Preparatory study
for the Bible illustration
of The Ascension of
Christ
c. 1848
Pen and ink
Fitzwilliam Museum

14 Design for the ceiling
of the billiard room at
no. 30 Westbourne
Terrace, London
c. 1848
Water-colour
*Victoria and Albert
Museum, 408–1895*

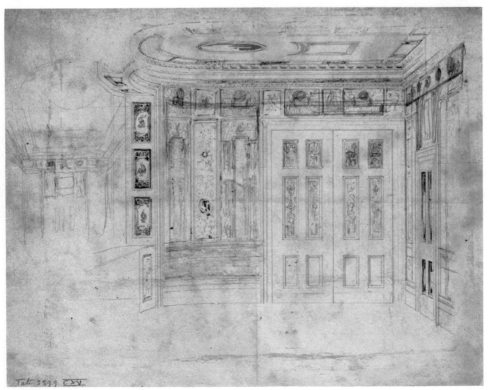

15 Sketch design for
the decoration of the
billiard room at no. 30
Westbourne Terrace,
London
c. 1848
Pen, pencil and water-
colour
*Victoria and Albert
Museum, E.289–1975*

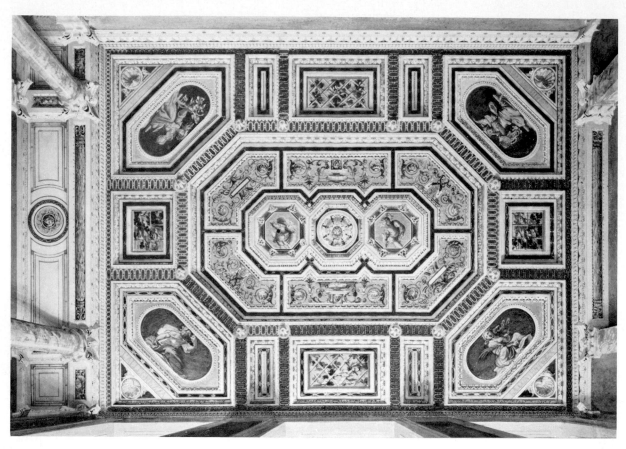

16 Design for the
dining-room ceiling at
Deysbrook House
c. 1847
Water-colour
*Victoria and Albert
Museum, 8586A*

17 Preparatory studies
for the figure of
'Thankfulness' in the
drawing-room at
Deysbrook House
c. 1847
Red chalk
*Victoria and Albert
Museum, D.2074–1885*

24

18 Design for a
candlestick
c. 1847–8
Pen and pencil
*Victoria and Albert
Museum, E.2097–1911*

19 Hot air stove made
by Hoole and Company
1851
*Victoria and Albert
Museum, 4030–1853*

20 Designs for knives
for George Wostenholm
1851
Walker Art Gallery

25

21 Design for a stove
for Hoole and Company
1857
Pen and ink, and wash
*National Gallery of
Victoria, Melbourne*

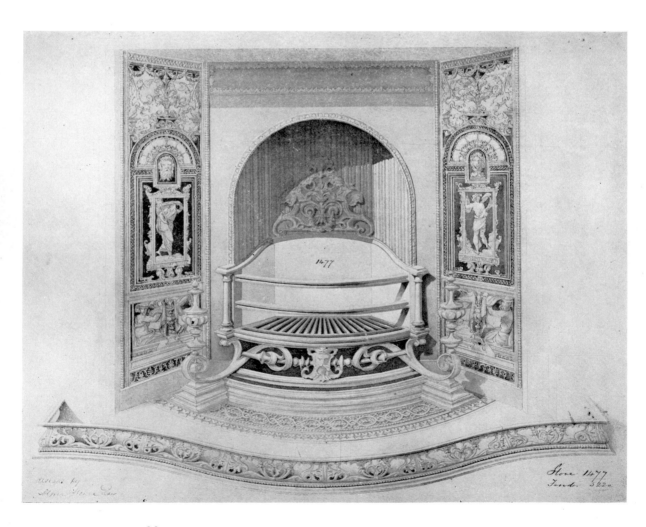

22 The 'Pluto and
Proserpine' grate made
by Hoole and Company
1855
*Victoria and Albert
Museum, 8532–1863*

23 Design for a stove
with male figures for
Hoole and Company
1852–3
Pen and ink, and wash
*National Gallery of
Victoria, Melbourne*

27

24, 25 Designs for a pair
of tile panels for a stove
for Hoole and Company
1852–3
Blue wash
*National Gallery of
Victoria, Melbourne*

26 The 'Festoon'
chimney-piece, made by
the Coalbrookdale Iron
Company
c. 1856
Engraving
*Royal Institute of
British Architects*

27 Paired pilaster
chimney-piece, made by
the Coalbrookdale Iron
Company
c. 1856
Lithograph
*Royal Institute of
British Architects*

28 Design for a silver
ewer
Pen, pencil and wash
*Victoria and Albert
Museum, E.2094–1911*

29 Design for a lamp
standard
Pen, pencil and wash
*Victoria and Albert
Museum, E.2105–1911*

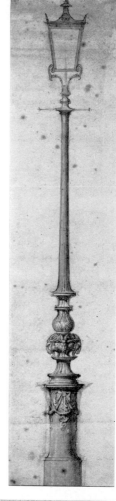

30 Large vase made by
Minton and Company
c. 1861
*Victoria and Albert
Museum, 184–1864*

31 Design for a majolica
teapot
Pencil and water-colour
*Victoria and Albert
Museum, E.2693–1911*

32 Portrait of Leonard
William Collmann
c. 1854
Oil on canvas
Fogg Art Museum, USA

33 Portrait of Mary Ann
Collmann
c. 1854
Oil on canvas
Tate Gallery

34 Design for the
decoration of the
boudoir at Daylesford
House
c. 1853–4
Pencil and water-colour
*Victoria and Albert
Museum, E.78–1975*

35 Design for the
decoration of the Italian
Court at the Crystal
Palace at Sydenham
1852–3
Pen and pencil
Tate Gallery

36 Design, stained by
water, for the decoration
of the Royal waiting-
room at Paddington
Station
1854
Pen, pencil, gold leaf
and water-colour
*Royal Institute of
British Architects*

37 King Alfred and His
Mother
c. 1848
Oil on panel
Fine Art Society

38 Working drawing
for the figure of 'Amoret'
for the drawing-room at
no. 11 Kensington
Palace Gardens, London
1855
Pencil
*Royal Institute of
British Architects*

35

40 Design for the front
façade of the Sheffield
School of Art
1854
Pencil and water-colour
*Royal Institute of
British Architects*

41 Architectural
composition
c. 1845
Pencil, pen and ink, and
water-colour
*Royal Institute of
British Architects*

42 The Wellington
Monument in St Paul's
Cathedral in 1911
*From a photograph in the
MacColl Collection,
Victoria and Albert
Museum Library*

43 Plaster model of the
sarcophagus and base of
the Wellington
Monument
*Victoria and Albert
Museum, 321–1878*

44 Full size plaster
model of 'Valour and
Cowardice', Wellington
Monument
*Victoria and Albert
Museum, 321B–1878*

45 Preparatory study
for the figure of 'Valour',
Wellington Monument
Red chalk
*Victoria and Albert
Museum, D.1232–1907*

46 Preparatory study
for the figure of 'Truth',
Wellington Monument
Red chalk
*National Gallery of
Victoria, Melbourne*

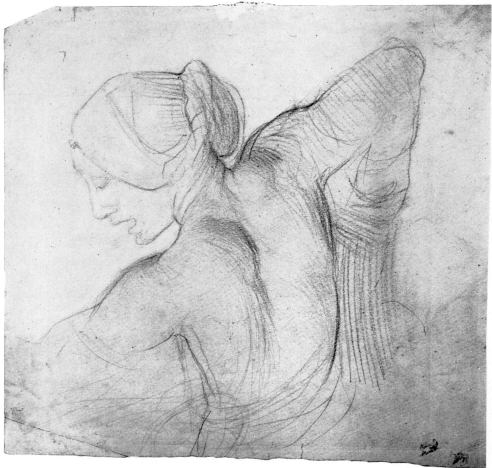

38

39

48 Design for the north, buffet-wall of the dining-room at Dorchester House
c. 1860
Pencil, pen and water-colour
Victoria and Albert Museum, E.354–1975

49 Cartoon for the panel 'The Judgement of Paris' proposed for the dining-room ceiling at Dorchester House
c. 1860
Oil on canvas
Victoria and Albert Museum, P.2–1975

50 One of the pair of
doors onto the gallery,
Dorchester House
Walker Art Gallery

51 Plaster model for a
door roundel at
Dorchester House
c. 1860
*Victoria and Albert
Museum*

52 Detail from a sheet
of preliminary studies
for the caryatids of the
dining-room chimney-
piece at Dorchester
House
Pencil
*Royal Institute of
British Architects*

53 Plaster model for a
Memorial to the Great
Exhibition of 1851
*Victoria and Albert
Museum, 318–1880*

54 Preparatory studies
for the figures, Great
Exhibition Memorial
Red chalk
*Victoria and Albert
Museum, D.2067–1885*

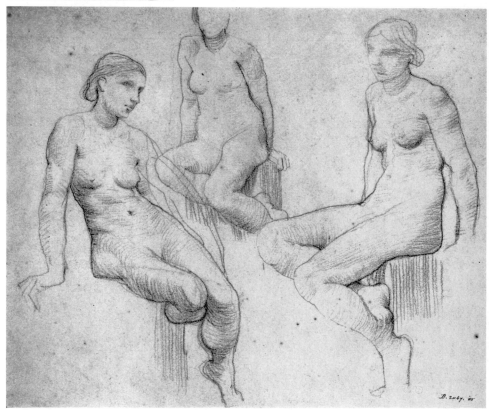

42

55 Stevens's house in Eton Road, Hampstead before demolition in 1964, when it was called Wellington House
Greater London Council

56 Interior of the library at Wellington House
From a photograph in the *Victoria and Albert Museum*

57 Wood and plaster
half model of the dome
of St Paul's Cathedral,
the proposed mosaic
decorations sketched in
oil
c. 1862–5
The model is in the
Trophy Room at
St Paul's

58 Detail of the model

59 Head of 'Daniel'. Trial mosaic panel for the decoration of one of the spandrels of the dome of St Paul's Cathedral
c. 1864
Victoria and Albert Museum, 108–1873

60 Preparatory study for the decoration of St Paul's Cathedral
c. 1862–9
Red chalk and pencil
Victoria and Albert Museum, E.2585–1911

61 Preparatory study for the decoration of St Paul's Cathedral
c. 1862–9
Red chalk
Victoria and Albert Museum, D.2083–1885

45

62 Sketch for a lunette
depicting 'The Angel
announcing the Birth of
Our Lord to the
Shepherds', for Christ
Church, Cosway Street,
London
c. 1862–5
Oil on board
Tate Gallery

63 Preliminary study
for the lunette, Christ
Church, Cosway Street,
London
c. 1862–5
Red chalk
Fogg Art Museum, USA

64 Sketch for the decoration of the Olympic Theatre, London
1863–4
Pencil and wash
Victoria and Albert Museum, E.2645–1911

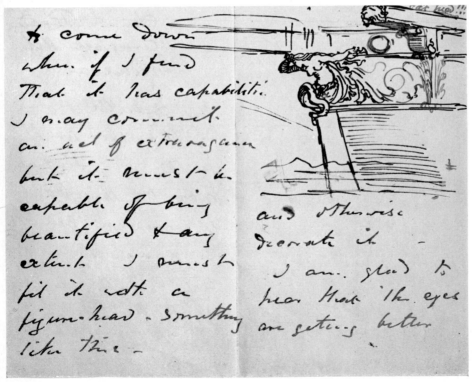

65 Sketch design, in a letter to Alfred Pegler, for the figure-head of a yacht
1864
Royal Institute of British Architects

47

66 Group of three
struggling figures
Cast in bronze from a
rough study in plaster
*Victoria and Albert
Museum, A.13–1975*

67 Wax model for a
National Prize Medal
for the Department of
Science and Art
1856
*Victoria and Albert
Museum, 7814–1863*

68 Design for a
certificate for the
International
Exhibition of 1862
Pencil
*Victoria and Albert
Museum, 2720*